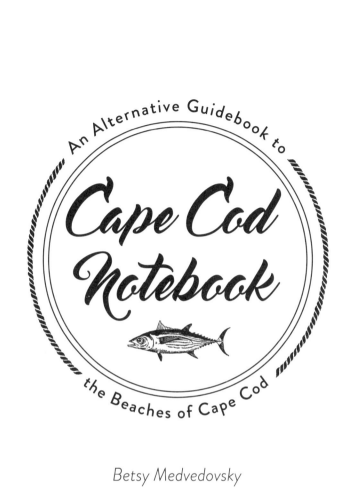

An Alternative Guidebook to

Cape Cod Notebook

the Beaches of Cape Cod

Betsy Medvedovsky

Schiffer Publishing Ltd

4880 Lower Valley Road • Atglen, PA 19310

Key

Every attempt has been made to be as accurate as possible with the current state of the beaches. If there are any updates, please share them by e-mailing Betsy at betsy@withandagainst.com.

GENERAL

 Salt Water

 Marshy

 Freshwater

 Large waves and/or strong currents

 Lifeguard

 Bathrooms or porta potties

 Showers

 Snack Bar

 Boardwalk

 Boat Ramp

 Playground

PARKING

 Sticker-only parking which must be purchased ahead of time. (Usually, stickers are available only to residents or long-term renters, but in some towns are available to visitors as well.)

P Free parking

P$ Paid parking available for non-residents, $15 or less

P$$ Paid parking available for non-residents, more than $15

ACCESSIBILITY

 Steep descent or stairs

 Beach wheelchair and/or Mobi-Chair available

 Cited by numerous sources as a handicap accessible beach

 Cited by most sources as a handicap accessible beach

OTHER

 Fire permits available (Limited supply; call ahead for more info.)

ORV Off-road vehicle permit available

 Popular beach

MAP ICONS

 Ferry departure point

Contents

Notes

HOW TO USE THIS NOTEBOOK

This is a guidebook, notebook, sketch pad, souvenir. It's a space for notes about the sunset, landscape or wildlife sketches, pleas to bring more snacks next year, or info on an ice cream shop a friend recommended. It's a reminder of all the beaches visited and the beaches left to explore. It can be the starting-off point for travel plans or a resource when all the neighborhood beaches become boring. This is a bare-bones guidebook for you to fill.

Organized by the Cape's four main regions (Upper Cape, Mid Cape, Lower Cape, Outer Cape), this guide introduces locations from west to east, and then as Route 6 curves at Brewster, Harwich, and Chatham, from south to north. The Upper Cape, closest to Boston, includes the towns of Bourne, Falmouth, Sandwich, and Mashpee. Mid Cape includes Barnstable, Yarmouth, and Dennis. At the Cape's elbow is the Lower Cape, which includes the towns of Brewster, Harwich, and Chatham. Finally, the Outer Cape includes Orleans, Eastham, Wellfleet, Truro, and Provincetown.

While every effort has been made to be as inclusive as possible. There are too many tiny neighborhood beaches, lakes, and ponds to include every beach on the cape.

Tread Lightly

Cape Cod is a stunning environment to visit and enjoy. But it's also a fragile ecosystem. Please enjoy the Cape with care. Follow existing paths wherever possible and avoid walking on fragile dunes. Be ready to pack out trash as needed. Follow local signage indicating what areas are closed—your footsteps might harm a wildlife habitat. Similarly, treat the people of Cape Cod with care. Stay off private land, park only where it's allowed and try walking, biking, or using a shuttle bus where possible to avoid contributing to traffic.

Bodies of Water

Water is what makes Cape Cod what it is—both literally and figuratively. One of the pleasures of getting to know the Cape is getting to know each of the bodies of water that surround it, and having a sense for how directly they affect the coastal lands—and your beach experience. There are also plenty of interior bodies of water to explore.

In general, high season on the Cape is July and August; many of the warm-water beaches haven't warmed up enough by June.

Vineyard and Nantucket Sound
Warmer water with calm waves. Some, though not all, have fantastic sand for laying on and playing with. These are often some of the best family friendly beaches.

Buzzards Bay
Warmer water, with calm waves. Again, a lot of family friendly beaches.

Cape Cod Bay
Warmer, calm water. The tides are very noticeable, however. Swimming is often only possible during high tide, with beach space disappearing. At low tide, tidal flats emerge for long expanses, making swimming difficult but perfect for little kids to play in the water.

Atlantic Ocean
Cold water with dramatic waves, often paired with wind-swept dunes.

Kettle Lakes and Ponds
Cape Cod is strewn with some 360 lakes and ponds. Most of these are kettle ponds formed about 18,000 years ago when the Laurentide ice sheet covering the Cape Cod area retreated. As it retreated, it left chunks of ice embedded in the ground. As these ice blocks slowly melted, they left depressions. Shallow impressions gradually filled with sediment, but deeper ones, which extended to groundwater level, became ponds and lakes. Over time, erosion has smoothed out the shorelines and now some of these kettle ponds have become quite circular (see Gull Pond in Wellfleet).

Handicapped Access

Accessibility means different things to different people. For some, a beach is accessible if there is handicapped parking and a handicapped restroom. Others require a Mobi-Chair for wheelchair access. And for others, none of these mean anything if there are steep dunes to traverse.

For this reason, the vague term of "handicapped accessible" is avoided here. In general, any known accessibility issues (i.e., steep dunes or stairs) are noted. Beaches that have been named in numerous sources as having good handicapped access are marked ♿ while beaches considered universally very accessible are marked ♿.

Beach Wheelchair Loaner Program

As a rule, beaches that are likely to be more accessible than others participate in this program and offer either beach wheelchairs or Mobi-chairs. If the beach you are planning to visit does not offer these, Smile Mass offers a loaner program for beach wheelchairs. Visit smilemass.org/loaner-program.html.

Handicapped Parking

Unless noted, handicapped parking is available wherever parking is available.

Resident-Only Beaches

Many guidebooks and websites will often refer to resident-only beaches. However, these restrictions only extend to whether non-resident parking is allowed. Any pedestrians and cyclists are welcome, though occasionally, they may be charged to enter.

Parking

In general, parking fills up during the prime months of July and August during lifeguard hours. This is especially true where parking is free and/or amenities are plentiful. Walk and bike wherever possible.

Acknowledgments

Thank you to Cathy Taylor, assistant director of Cape Organization for Rights of the Disabled (CORD), for scanning and sharing an accessibility guide to the Cape. Thank you also to Anna Medvedovsky for trips to the Cape and time brainstorming about what this notebook should include.

BOURNE

SANDWICH

MASHPEE

FALMOUTH

Upper Cape

Bourne

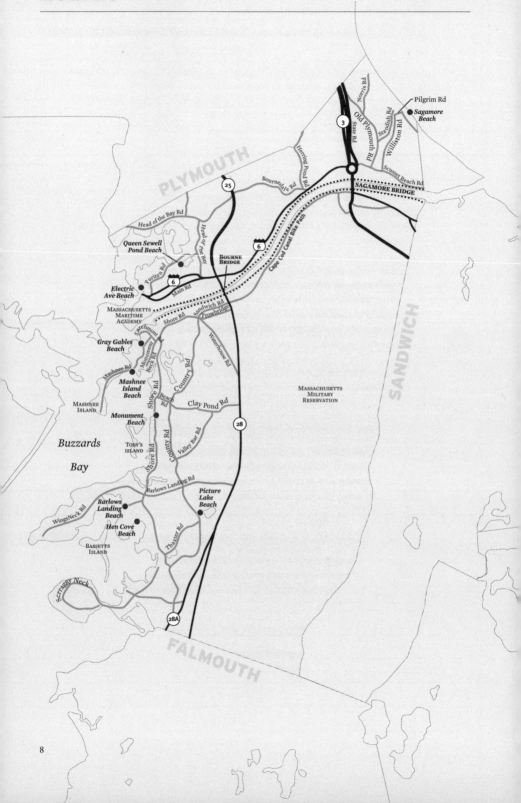

PLYMOUTH

Pilgrim Rd

Sagamore Beach

Norris Rd

Standish Rd

Williston Rd

Old Plymouth Rd

3

State Rd

Herring Pond Rd

Bournedale Rd

25

Scusset Beach Rd

SAGAMORE BRIDGE

Cape Cod Canal Bike Path

Head of the Bay Rd

Queen Sewell Pond Beach

Head of the Bay

Puritan Rd

6

BOURNE BRIDGE

6

Main Rd

Electric Ave Beach

MASSACHUSETTS MARITIME ACADEMY

Sandwich Rd

Shore Rd

Trowbridge

Patchmont Rd

Gray Gables Beach

Monument Neck Rd

Mashnee Rd

Country Rd

Waterhouse Rd

SANDWICH

Mashnee Island Beach

Shore Rd

Beach Rd

Clay Pond Rd

MASSACHUSETTS MILITARY RESERVATION

MASHNEE ISLAND

Monument Beach

County Rd

Valley Bar Rd

Buzzards Bay

TOBY'S ISLAND

28

Shore Rd

Barlows Landing Rd

Picture Lake Beach

Wings Neck Rd

Barlows Landing Beach

County Rd

Hen Cove Beach

Thaxter Rd

BASSETTS ISLAND

Scraggy Neck

28A

FALMOUTH

Parking — All of Bourne's beaches require a town parking sticker, except for Scusset Beach, which is state owned. A proof of residency along with a proof of your length of stay in Bourne will be required; only those staying in Bourne for a week or longer are eligible.

Dogs — Allowed on beaches from October 16 through April 30.

Natural Resources Office
Town Hall
24 Perry Ave
508.759.0621, ext. 3

Barlows Landing Beach

Off Route 28, Bourne • Pocasset Harbor, Buzzards Bay • 508.759.0621

Electric Avenue Beach

Electric Avenue, Bourne • Buzzards Bay • 508.759.0621

 *View of the wind turbine. Good sand.*

Gray Gables Beach

Gilder Road, Gray Gables Village, Bourne • Buzzards Bay • 508.759.0621

   View of boats in the harbor. Features kid-friendly rivulets at low tide.

Hen Cove Beach

Circuit Street, Bourne • Hen Cove, Buzzards Bay • 508.759.0621

Mashnee Island Beach

Mashnee Island, Bourne • Phinney's Harbor, off Buzzards Bay • 508.759.0621

 No parking.

Monument Beach

Shore Road, Bourne • Buzzards Bay • 508.759.0621

Call 508.759.0613 to reserve.

Picture Lake Beach

Old County Road, Bourne • 508.759.0621

   No handicap parking.

Queen Sewell Pond Beach

Cherry Street, Bourne • 508.759.0621

  Intermittently closed due to algal bloom.

Sagamore Beach

Standish Road, Bourne • Cape Cod Bay • 508.759.0621

Sandwich

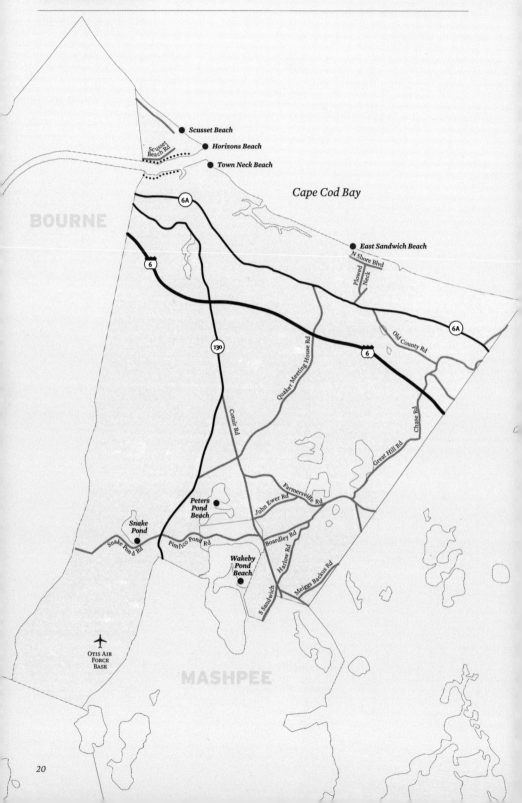

Scusset Beach

Horizons Beach

Scusset Beach Rd

Town Neck Beach

Cape Cod Bay

6A

BOURNE

6

East Sandwich Beach

N Shore Blvd

Plowed Neck

6A

Old County Rd

6

130

Quaker Meeting House Rd

Cotuit Rd

Chase Rd

Great Hill Rd

Farmersville Rd

Peters
Pond
Beach

John Ewer Rd

Snake
Pond

Boardley Rd

Snake Pond Rd

Pimlico Pond Rd

Wakeby
Pond
Beach

Hazlow Rd

Meiggs Backus Rd

S Sandwich

OTIS AIR
FORCE
BASE

MASHPEE

NOTES

The Sandy Neck beach straddles both Sandwich and Barnstable, but is under Barnstable in this book.

Dogs — From May 15 to September 15, dogs are prohibited on any public beach or dune.

STICKERS + MORE INFO
TAX COLLECTOR'S OFFICE
Town Hall Annex
145 Main St
508.759.0621

East Sandwich Beach

North Shore Boulevard, East Sandwich • Cape Cod Bay • 508.888.4361

     Call 508.888.0525 to reserve.

Horizons Beach

Town Neck Road, Sandwich • Cape Cod Bay • 508.888.4361

Peters Pond Beach

Sandy Neck Road, Sandwich • 508.888.4361

    No handicapped parking.

Scusset Beach

Scusset Beach Road, Scusset Beach State Reservation, Sandwich
Cape Cod Bay • 508.888.4361

Call 508.866.2580 to reserve wheelchair. Long walk from parking lot to beach.

Snake Pond

Snake Pond Road, Sandwich • 508.888.4361

Town Neck Beach

Town Neck Road, Sandwich • Cape Cod Bay • 508.888.4361

 *Call 508.888.0525 to reserve.*

Wakeby Pond Beach

South Sandwich Road, Sandwich • 508.888.4361

Falmouth

BOURNE

MASHPE

Megansett Beach

Wild Habror Rd

Old Main

Garnet

151

Curley Blvd

28

Quaker Rd

S. Turner Rd

Hatchville Rd

Boxberry Hill Rd

Old Silver Beach

Thomas Landers Rd

Hatchville Rd

Nashanena

Blacksmith Shop Rd

Deer Pond Rd

Carriage Shop Rd

Hayview

Currier Rd

Chapoquoit Beach

Chapoquoit

Old Dock

Brick Kiln Rd

Locustfield Rd

Gifford St

Sandwich Rd

Fresh Pond Rd

28A

28

Metoxit

Otoxit

Menauhant

FALMOUTH
AIRPORT

Buzzards

Wood Neck Beach

Ter Heun Dr

Grews Pond Beach

Jones Rd

Gifford St

Sandwich Rd

Homestead

Shorewood Dr

Acapesket Rd

Davisville Rd

Old Main Rd

WASHBURN
ISLAND

Sippewisset Rd

Bay

Woods Hole Rd

Mill Rd

Shore Rd

Clinton

Scranton

Falmouth Ave

Marravista Ave

Menauhant Rd

Menauhant Beach

Quisett Rd

School St

Woods Hole Rd

Lillie

Oyster Pond

Surf Dr

Shining Sea Bikeway

Surf Drive Beach

Trunk River Beach

Grand

Falmouth Heights Beach

Bristol Beach

Church Rd

▲ *NOBSKA
POINT LIGHT*

Vineyard Sound

NOTES
Falmouth's parking fees are in effect from mid-June to mid-September.

Dogs — Allowed on beaches from October 1 through April 1.

Handicap Wheelchairs — The beach wheelchair icon marks where beach wheelchairs are readily available; beach wheelchairs are available at any beach with advance notice.

STICKERS + MORE INFO
BEACH COMMITTEE
Ellen T. Mitchell Bath House
56 Surf Drive, Falmouth
508.548.8623

Bristol Beach

Menauhant Road, Falmouth • Vineyard Sound • 508.548.8623

Chapoquoit Beach

Chapoquoit Road, West Falmouth • Buzzards Bay • 508.548.8623

Falmouth Heights Beach

Grand Avenue and Central Park Avenue, Falmouth • Vineyard Sound • 508.548.8623

 *(some stairs)*

Grews Pond Beach

Goodwill Park, off Gifford Street, Falmouth • 508.584.8623

Megansett Beach

County Road, Falmouth • Megansett Harbor, off Buzzards Bay • 508.548.8623

Menauhant Beach

Menauhant Road, East Falmouth • Vineyard Sound • 508.548.8623

Old Silver Beach

Quaker Road, North Falmouth • Buzzards Bay • 508.548.8623

Surf Drive Beach

Surf Drive Road, Falmouth Village • Vineyard Sound • 508.548.8623

Trunk River Beach

Woods Hole, Falmouth • Vineyard Sound • 508.548.8623

Wood Neck Beach

Wood Neck Road, Sippewisett, Falmouth • Buzzards Bay • 508.548.8623

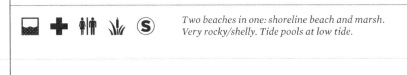

Two beaches in one: shoreline beach and marsh.
Very rocky/shelly. Tide pools at low tide.

Mashpee

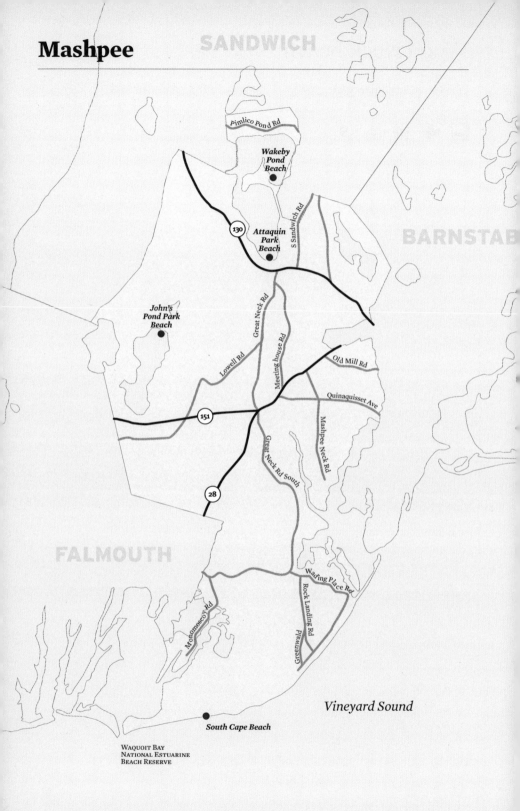

SANDWICH

BARNSTAB

FALMOUTH

Pimlico Pond Rd

Wakeby Pond Beach

130

Attaquin Park Beach

S Sandwich Rd

John's Pond Park Beach

Great Neck Rd

Meeting house Rd

Lowell Rd

Old Mill Rd

Quinaquisset Ave

151

Mashpee Neck Rd

Great Neck Rd South

28

Wading Place Rd

Rock Landing Rd

Greenwald

Monomoscoi Rd

Vineyard Sound

South Cape Beach

Waquoit Bay
National Estuarine
Beach Reserve

YARM

NOTES
The only beach where non-residents can park is the
state-run South Cape Beach.

Dogs — Dogs are not allowed on beaches.

STICKERS + MORE INFO
OFFICE OF TOWN CLERK
16 Great Neck Road North
508.539.1400

Attaquin Park Beach

Lake Avenue, off Route 130, Mashpee • 508.539.1400

John's Pond Park Beach

Back Road, Mashpee • 508.539.1400

South Cape Beach

Great Oak Road, Mashpee • Vineyard Sound • 508.539.1400

To reserve beach chair, call 508.457.0495.
South Cape Beach has two lots: a town lot for residents
and a state lot that non-residents can use. Use the
state-managed lot for beach wheelchair accessibility.

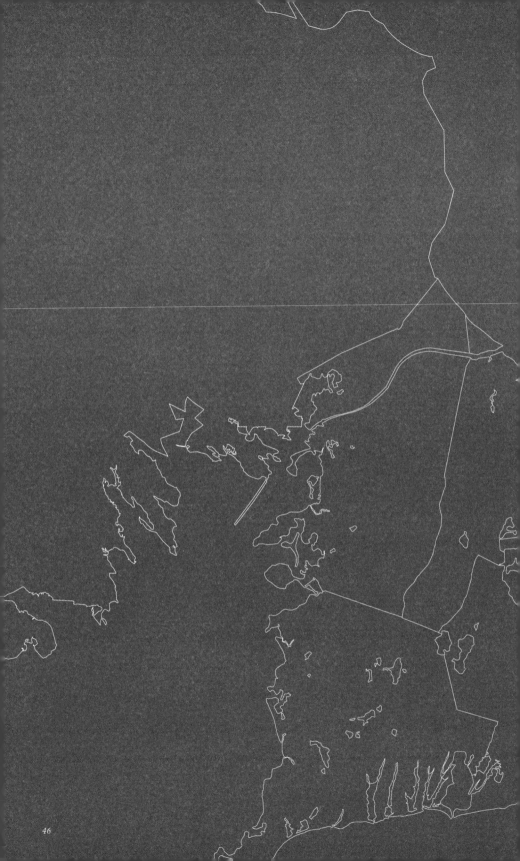

Mid Cape

Barnstable

CAPE COD BAY

Sandy Neck Beach

SANDY NECK

SANDY NECK LIGHT

SANDWICH

GREAT MARSHES

Barnstable Harbor

Millway Beach

Sandy Neck Rd

High St

Cedar St

Maple St

6

Meetinghouse Rd

Church St

Parker Rd

Plum St

Oak St

Main St

6A

Millway

Commerce Rd

Indian Neck Trail

Mary Dunn Rd

Kewney

CAPE COD AIRPORT

Phinney's Ln

Jail Ln

Hathaway's Pond Beach

Kidd's Hill

Independence Dr

Race La

School St

Mystic Lake

Middle Lake

Hamblin Pond Beach

Old Falmouth Rd

Old Stage Rd

Hill Rd

Wequaquet Lake Beach

Wequaquet Lake

Higgins Neck Rd

Old

Attucks Ln

Strawberry Hill Rd

Bearse's

132

BARNSTABLE AIRPORT

Yarmouth Rd

Wakeby Rd

Old Post Rd

149

Old

Barnstable Rd

Great Marsh Rd

Phinney's Ln

W Main

Lincoln Rd

Pitcher's Way

Way

Barnstable Rd

Main St

Lovells Pond Beach

28

S County Rd

W

Bumps River Rd

St

Old Craigsville Rd

Pine St

Old Town Rd

Scudder Ave

North St

South St

Old Colony

Ocean St

Veterans Park Beach

Putnam Ave

Little River

Old Post Rd

Pond St

Old Mill Rd

Swift Ave

Sea Grand La

Bay Lane

S Main

St

Craigsville Beach Rd

W Main

Sea St

Gosnold St

Kalmus Park Beach

North Bay

Joshua Pond Beach

Main St

E Bay Rd

Craigsville Beach

Covell Beach

SQUAW ISLAND

Long Beach

HYANNIS POINT

Ocean Ave

Eugenia Fortes (East) Beach

Orrin Keyes (Sea St) Beach

HYANNIS LIGHTHOUSE

Samsit

Main St

School St

Cotuit Bay

OSTERVILLE GRAND ISLAND

West Bay

DEAD NECK ISLAND

Parker Rd

Wianno Ave

Dowses Beach

View Ave

Sea

SAMPSONS ISLAND SANCTUARY

NANTUCKET SOUND

Loop Beach

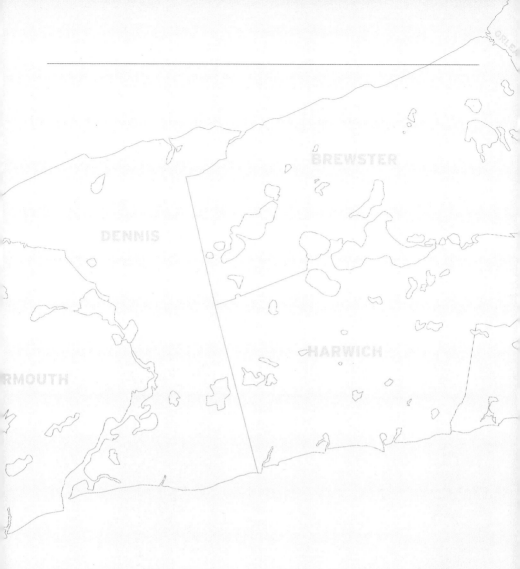

NOTES
Parking Fees — In effect from Memorial Day through Labor Day, 9AM–3:45PM.

Dogs — Allowed on beaches from September 16 through May 14.

Camp Fires — Allowed on the Sandy Neck ORV beach after 7PM under appropriate weather conditions. Call ahead for info: 508.362.8300.

Smoking — Prohibited on public beaches from May 15 through September 15.

STICKERS + MORE INFO
YOUTH & COMMUNITY CENTER
141 Bassett Lane, Hyannis
508.362.4795

Covell Beach

Craigsville Beach Road, Centerville • Nantucket Sound • 508.790.6345

Craigsville Beach

Craigsville Beach Road, Centerville • Nantucket Sound • 508.790.6345

 *(snack bars across street)*

Dowses Beach

348 E. Bay Road, Osterville • Nantucket Sound • 508.420.2403

    No ball playing rule. Lots of seashells.

Eugenia Fortes (East) Beach

Iyanough Ave, off Marstons Ave, Hyannisport • Nantucket Sound • 508.790.6345

 (S) *Lots of shells.*

Hamblin Pond Beach

Route 149, Marstons Mills, Barnstable • 508.420.1862

Hathaway's Pond Beach

Phinney's Lane, Barnstable • 508.362.8159

Joshua Pond Beach

Tower Hill Road, Osterville • 508.420.1862

Kalmus Park Beach

670 Ocean Street, Hyannis, Barnstable • Nantucket Sound • 508.790.9884

Divided between swimmers and windsurfers. Shelly sand.

Long Beach

Long Beach Road, Centerville, Barnstable • Nantucket Sound • 508.790.6345

    Lots of shells.

Loop Beach

Ocean View Avenue, Cotuit, Barnstable • Nantucket Sound • 508.420.2405

Lovells Pond Beach

Santuit-Newtown Road, Cotuit, Barnstable • 508.420.5763

Millway Beach

Phinney's Lane, Barnstable • Cape Cod Bay • 508.362.4795

Orrin Keyes (Sea Street) Beach

175 Ocean Ave., Hyannis, Barnstable • Nantucket Sound • 508.790.9886

 *No handicapped parking.*

Sandy Neck Beach

Sandy Neck Road, West Barnstable • Cape Cod Bay • 508.362.8300

Veterans Park Beach

480 Ocean Street, Hyannis, Barnstable • Lewis Bay, off Nantucket Sound • 508.790.9885

Wequaquet Lake Beach

Shootflying Hill Road, Centerville, Barnstable • 508.362.5953

Yarmouth

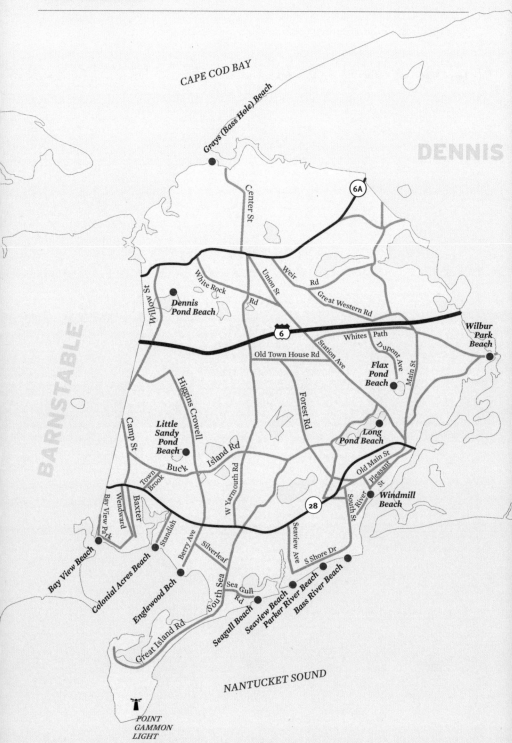

CAPE COD BAY

DENNIS

Grays (Bass Hole) Beach

6A

Center St

Willow St

White Rock

Dennis Pond Beach

Union St

Weir Rd

Great Western Rd

Whites Path

Dupont Ave

Wilbur Park Beach

6

Old Town House Rd

Station Ave

Flax Pond Beach

Main St

BARNSTABLE

Higgins Crowell

Camp St

Little Sandy Pond Beach

Island Rd

Buck

W Yarmouth Rd

Forest Rd

Long Pond Beach

Old Main St

Pleasant St

Windmill Beach

River

Town Brook

28

South St

Bay View Park

Wendward

Baxter

Standish

Berry Ave

Silverleaf

Seaview Ave

S Shore Dr

Bay View Beach

Colonial Acres Beach

Englewood Bch

South Sea Rd

Sea Gull Rd

Seagull Beach

Seaview Beach

Parker River Beach

Bass River Beach

Great Island Rd

NANTUCKET SOUND

POINT GAMMON LIGHT

NOTES
Parking Fees — In effect from Memorial Day through Labor Day.

Dogs — Not allowed on any beaches.

Smoking — Not allowed on any beaches.

STICKERS + MORE INFO
Yarmouth Beach Office
Town Hall
1146 Route 28
South Yarmouth
508.398.2231

Bass River Beach

South Shore Drive, South Yarmouth • Nantucket Sound • 508.398.2231

Bay View Beach

Bay View Street, off Rt. 28, Yarmouth • Lewis Bay, off Nantucket Sound • 508.398.2231

Right next to the marina, which can be a plus or minus.
Great point to watch the 4th of July fireworks.

Colonial Acres Beach

Standish Road, Yarmouth • 508.398.2231

 *A little far from parking.*

Dennis Pond Beach

Summer Street, Yarmouthport • 508.398.2231

  Summer Street off Willow Street has deep potholes: watch out.

Englewood Beach

Berry Avenue, West Yarmouth • Lewis Bay, off Nantucket Sound • 508.398.2231

 *(very limited parking)*

Flax Pond Beach

Dupont Avenue, South Yarmouth • 508.398.2231

 *No sand. Pine shaded area. Tennis and basketball courts.*

Grays (Bass Hole) Beach

Center Street, Yarmouthport • Cape Cod Bay • 508.398.2231

Watch out for bugs at dusk. Boardwalk extends only partly to the beach.

Little Sandy Pond Beach

Buck Island Road, Sandy Pond Recreation Area, West Yarmouth • 508.398.2231

 *Softball field, basketball court, soccer field nearby.*

Long Pond (Wings Grove) Beach

Long Pond Drive, South Yarmouth • 508.398.2231

Parker River Beach (Beachwood Beach)

South Shore Drive, South Yarmouth • Nantucket Sound • 508.398.2231

 *(some stairs)*

Seagull Beach

Sea Gull Beach Road, West Yarmouth • Nantucket Sound • 508.398.2231

Seaview Beach

South Shore Drive, South Yarmouth • Nantucket Sound • 508.398.2231

🏖 ✚ 🚻 🚶 P$ 🪜 *Watch out for jellyfish.*

Wilbur Park Beach

High Bank Road, South Yarmouth • 508.398.2231

    *Tiny beach, mostly for boat launches. Very shelly.*

Windmill Beach

River Street, Yarmouth • 508.398.2231

Dennis

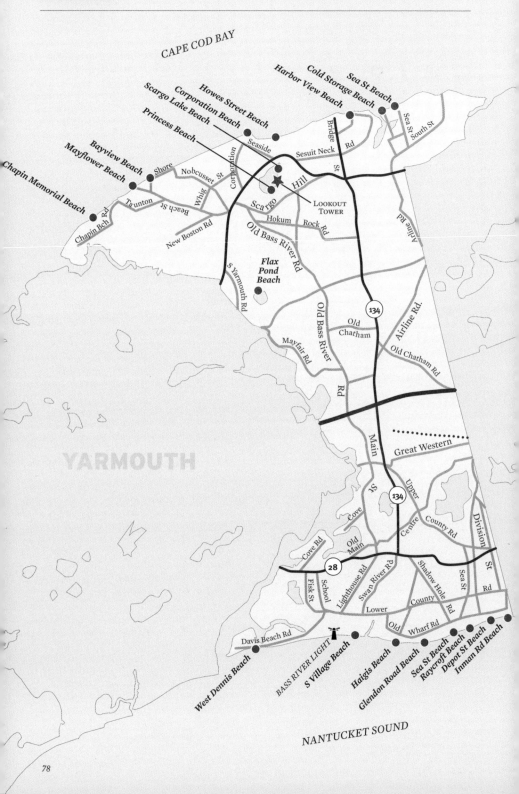

CAPE COD BAY

Chapin Memorial Beach

Mayflower Beach
Bayview Beach

Princess Beach
Scargo Lake Beach
Corporation Beach
Howes Street Beach

Harbor View Beach
Cold Storage Beach
Sea St Beach

Chapin Bch Rd

Shore
Taunton
Nobcusset St
Whig
Beach St
Corporation
Seaside
New Boston Rd

Sesuit Neck

Bridge St

Sea St South St

Scargo Hill

Hokum Rock Rd

LOOKOUT TOWER

Old Bass River Rd

Flax Pond Beach

S Yarmouth Rd

Mayfair Rd

Old Bass River

Old Chatham

134

Airline Rd.

Old Chatham Rd

YARMOUTH

Great Western

Main St

Upper

134

Cowe

Centre

County Rd

Division St

Rd

Cove Rd

Old Main

Lighthouse Rd

Swan River Rd

Shadow Hole Rd

Sea St

Rd

28

Fisk St

School

Lower

County

Old Wharf Rd

Davis Beach Rd

BASS RIVER LIGHT

West Dennis Beach

S Village Beach

Haigis Beach

Glendon Road Beach

Sea St Beach
Raycroft Beach
Depot St Beach
Inman Rd Beach

NANTUCKET SOUND

NOTES

Parking Fees — In effect Memorial Day through Labor Day (5PM).

Dogs — Not allowed from the Friday before Memorial Day through Labor Day.

STICKERS + MORE INFO

Dennis Beach Office
465 Route 134
South Dennis
508.760.6159

Sticker Hours
April–Memorial Day Weekend
M–F: 9AM–4PM

Memorial Day Weekend–
Labor Day Weekend
M–F: 9AM–4PM
Sun: 9AM–12PM

BREWSTER

HARWICH

CHATHAM

Bayview Beach

Bayview Road, Dennis • Cape Cod Bay • 508.760.6159

Chapin Memorial Beach

Chapin Beach Road, off Rt. 6A, Dennis • Cape Cod Bay • 508.394.8300

P$$ ORV *Bit of a walk through the sand to the beach with an up and down part. Some rocks.*

Cold Storage Beach

Cold Storage Road, East Dennis • Cape Cod Bay • 508.760.6159

Corporation Beach

Corporation Road, off Rt. 6A, Dennis • Cape Cod Bay • 508.760.6159

Depot Street Beach

Depot Street, Dennis Port • Nantucket Sound • 508.760.6159

No parking and no amenities.

Glendon Road Beach

Old Wharf Road, Dennis Port • Nantucket Sound • 508.760.6159

Haigis Beach

Old Wharf Road, Dennis Port • Nantucket Sound • 508.760.6159

Harbor View Beach

Harbor Road, Dennis • Cape Cod Bay • 508.780.6159

Howes Street Beach

Howes Street, Dennis • Cape Cod Bay • 508.760.6159

Inman Road Beach

Inman Road, Dennis Port • Nantucket Sound • 508.760.6159

Mayflower Beach

Dunes Road, Dennis • Cape Cod Bay • 508.760.6159

Princess Beach

Scargo Hill Road, Dennis • Scargo Lake • 508.760.6159

 *Close to the Scargo Tower.*

Raycroft Beach

Raycroft Parkway, Dennis • Nantucket Sound • 508.760.6159

Scargo Lake Beach

Dr. Lord Road, Dennis • 508.760.6159

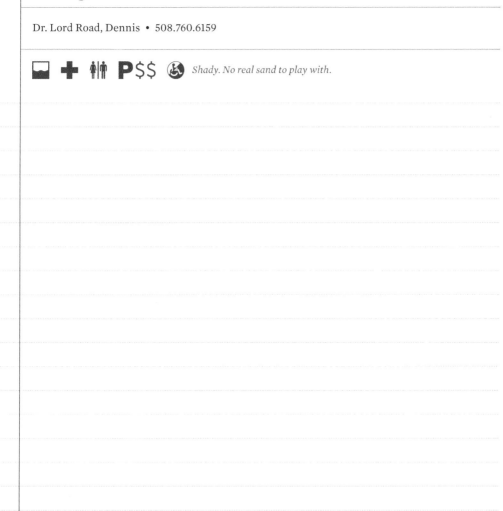 $ $$ *Shady. No real sand to play with.*

Sea Street Beach (Dennis Port)

Sea Street, Dennis Port • Nantucket Sound • 508.760.6159

Sea Street Beach (East Dennis)

Sea Street, off Rt. 6A, East Dennis • Cape Cod Bay • 508.760.6159

South Village Beach

South Village Road, Dennis Port • Nantucket Sound • 508.760.6159

West Dennis Beach

Davis Beach Road, West Dennis • Nantucket Sound • 508.760.6159

Lower Cape

BREWSTER

HARWICH

CHATHAM

Harwich

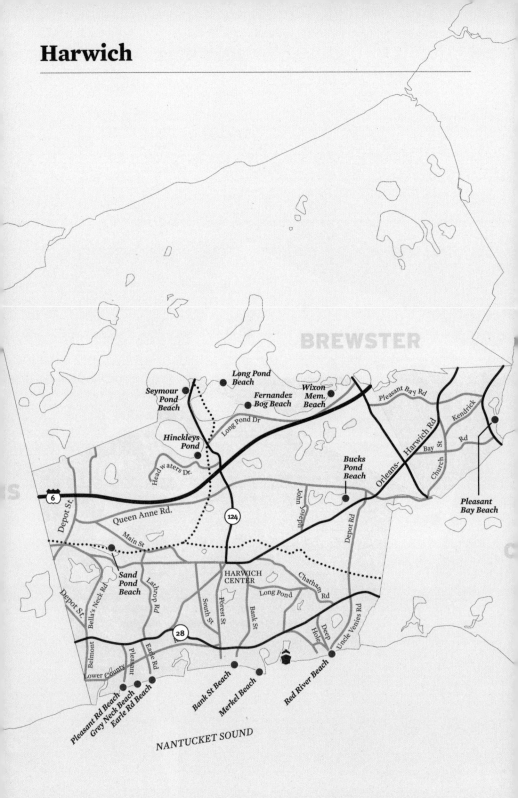

BREWSTER

Long Pond Beach

Seymour Pond Beach

Fernandez Bog Beach

Wixon Mem. Beach

Pleasant Bay Rd

Kendrick Rd

Long Pond Dr

Hinckleys Pond

Headwaters Dr.

Bucks Pond Beach

Orleans- Harwich Rd

Bay St

Church St

Pleasant Bay Beach

6

Depot St.

Queen Anne Rd.

124

John Joseph

Main St

Depot Rd

Sand Pond Beach

HARWICH CENTER

Chatham Rd

Bella's Neck Rd

Lathrop Rd

Long Pond

Depot St.

South St

Forest St

Bank St

Deep Hole

Uncle Venies Rd

28

Belmont

Pleasant

Earle Rd

Lower County

Bank St Beach

Merkel Beach

Red River Beach

Pleasant Rd Beach

Grey Neck Beach

Earle Rd Beach

NANTUCKET SOUND

NOTES

Parking Fees — In effect from mid-June through Labor Day.

Parking Stickers — Visitors can buy one- and two-week stickers with proof of temporary Harwich residency.

Parking stickers can be bought at several locations, listed on the right.

Dogs — Allowed from Labor Day through Memorial Day. During the summer, dogs may be walked in the **parking lot area only** at Red River Beach only, from dawn–9:00AM and from 4:30PM–dusk.

MORE INFO
Harwich Recreation
100 Oak Street
508.430.7553

STICKERS
Community Center
100 Oak Street
508.432.7638
M-Sun: 8AM–3PM

Chamber of Commerce
(with added $3 convenience fee)
June 22–Labor Day
1 Schoolhouse Road, Harwich Port
508.432.1600
M–F: 9AM–5PM
Sat: 10AM–4PM
Sun: 10AM–2PM

Harwich Town Hall
June 8–Labor Day
732 Main Street
508.430.7501
Mon: 8:30AM–8PM
Tu–Thu: 8:30AM–4PM
Fri: 8:30AM–noon

Chatham Harbor

Bank Street Beach

Bank Street, Harwich Port • Nantucket Sound • 508.430.7553

Bucks Pond Beach

Bucks Pond Road, off Rt. 39, Harwich • Bucks Pond • 508.430.7553

  No handicapped parking.

Earle Road Beach

Earle Road, Harwich • Nantucket Sound • 508.430.7553

Fernandez Bog Beach/Long Pond Beach

Long Pond Road, Harwich • Long Pond • 508.430.7553

Grey Neck Beach

Grey Neck Road, Harwich • Nantucket Sound • 508.430.7553

Hinckleys Pond

Hinckleys Pond, Harwich • 508.430.7553

 No parking.

Pleasant Road Beach

Pleasant Road, Harwich • Nantucket Sound • 508.430.7553

Red River Beach

Uncle Venies Road, Harwich Port • Nantucket Sound • 508.430.7553

Sand Pond Beach

Great Western Road, Harwich • 508.430.7553

Seymour Pond Beach

580 Pleasant Lake Ave, Rt. 124, Harwich • 508.430.7501

Wixon Memorial Beach

Cahoon Road, Harwich • Long Pond • 508.430.7553

 *Restroom is not accessible.*

Chatham

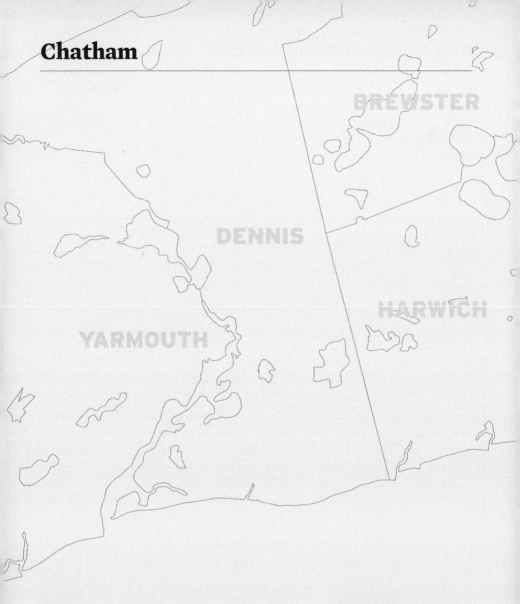

BREWSTER

DENNIS

HARWICH

YARMOUTH

NOTES
Parking Fees — In effect from mid-June through Labor Day.

Smoking — Prohibited on public beaches.

Dogs — Not allowed May 1–September 15 in beach areas. The only exception is Pleasant Bay/Jackknife Beach; dogs are allowed on the beach before 9AM and after 6PM.

Lifeguards — On duty from 9AM–4:30PM.

MORE INFO
Parks & Recreation
Chatham Community
Center
702 Main St.
508.945.5158

STICKERS
**Sticker Office
(For Residents)**
261 George Ryder Road
508.945.5180
Call ahead for hours

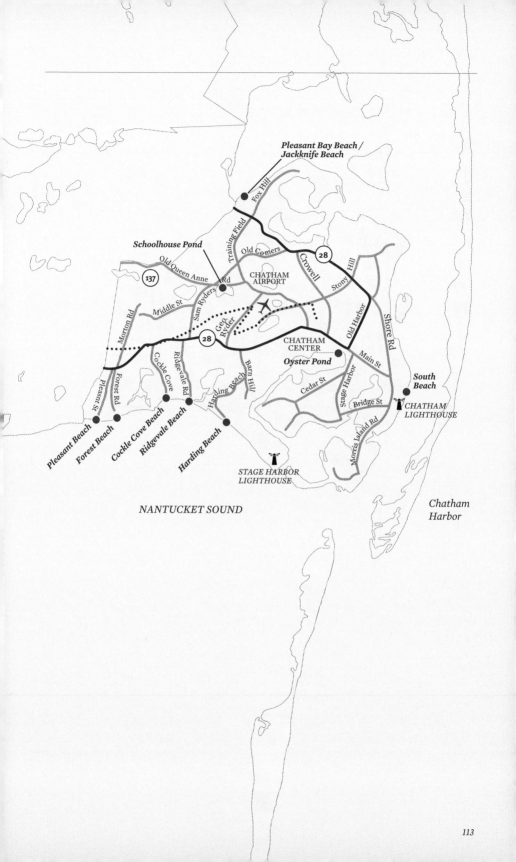

Pleasant Bay Beach / Jackknife Beach

Fox Hill

Training Field

Schoolhouse Pond

Old Queen Anne

Old Comers

Crowell

28

Stony Hill

137

CHATHAM AIRPORT

Sam Ryders Rd

Middle St

Morton Rd

Geo Ryder

28

CHATHAM CENTER

Oyster Pond

Old Harbor

Shore Rd

Main St

South Beach

Forest Rd

Pleasant St

Cockle Cove

Ridgevale Rd

Harding Beach

Barn Hill

Cedar St

Stage Harbor

Bridge St

CHATHAM LIGHTHOUSE

Pleasant Beach

Forest Beach

Cockle Cove Beach

Ridgevale Beach

Harding Beach

Morris Island Rd

STAGE HARBOR LIGHTHOUSE

NANTUCKET SOUND

Chatham Harbor

Cockle Cove Beach

Taylors Pond Road, off Cockle Cove Road, South Chatham • 508.945.5180

 *Windsurfing, kayaking.*

Forest Beach

Forest Road, off Rt. 28, South Chatham • Nantucket Sound • 508.945.5180

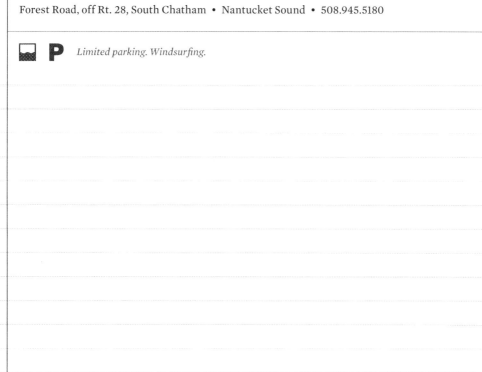 *Limited parking. Windsurfing.*

Harding Beach

Harding Beach Road, West Chatham • Nantucket Sound • 508.945.5180

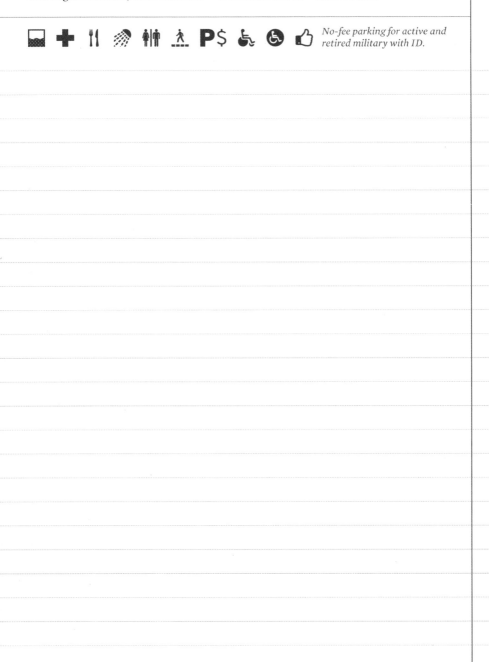

No-fee parking for active and retired military with ID.

Oyster Pond

Stage Harbor Road and Kingsbury Way, Chatham • Oyster River, off Nantucket Sound
508.945.5180

Pleasant Bay/Jackknife Beach

1296 Orleans Road, North Chatham • Pleasant Bay • 508.945.5180

 Dogs allowed before 9AM and after 6PM. Good kayaking.

Pleasant Beach

Pleasant Street, Chatham • Nantucket Sound • 508.945.5180

  Popular with windsurfers.

Ridgevale Beach

Ridgevale Road, Chatham • Nantucket Sound • 508.945.5180

Schoolhouse Pond

Schoolhouse Pond Road, West Chatham • 508.945.5180

South Beach (Chatham Light Beach)

Shore Road, by Chatham Light, Chatham • Atlantic Ocean • 508.945.5180

Seals. Parking limited to 30 min. For longer access, park in town and walk or take the shuttle. Strong currents and limited swimming. Watch for the red flag, which means swimming is prohibited.

Brewster

NOTES

All of Brewster's coastal beaches are on the bay; they offer incredibly expansive tidal flats at low tide.

Parking Fees — In effect from June 15 to Labor Day, 9AM to 3PM.

Stickers — All of the Brewster beaches are open to both residents and visitors **BUT** are sticker-parking only. That means that visitors must buy a day-pass at the Visitor Information Center, and only then can park.

Lifeguards — On duty from July 4th weekend through Labor Day weekend, 9AM–4PM at some lakes. None of the bay beaches have lifeguards.

Pets — Not allowed on public beaches between May 1 and October 1.

Accessibility — Besides a Mobi-Chair, which is permanently located at Long Pond, Brewster has a Mobi-Chair and a beach wheelchair available for loan. They are available at the Council on Aging with a requested donation of $10.

MORE INFO + STICKERS
Visitor Information Center
Brewster Town Offices
2198 Main Street
508.896.4511
9AM–3PM

BEACH WHEELCHAIRS
Council on Aging
1673 Main Street
508.896.2737
Mon-Fri: 8:30AM–4PM

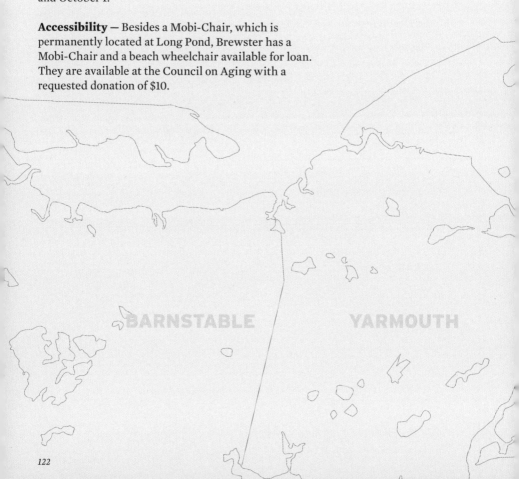

BARNSTABLE   YARMOUTH

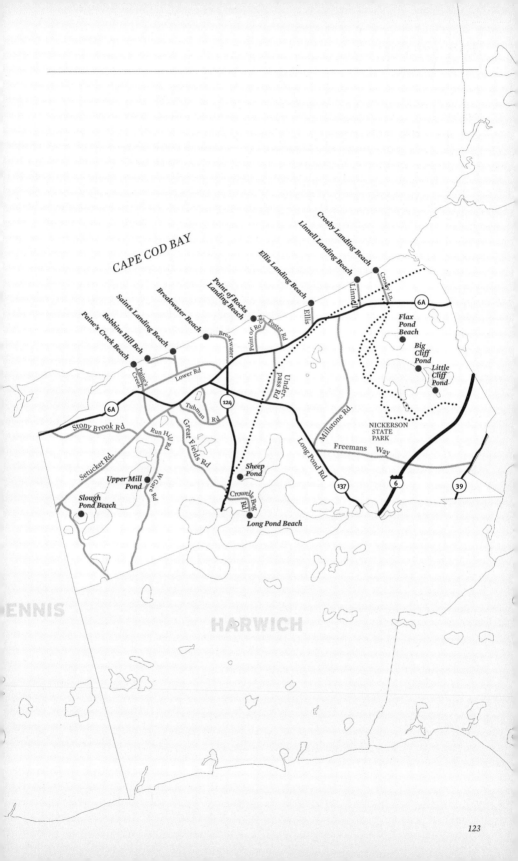

CAPE COD BAY

Crosby Landing Beach

Linnell Landing Beach

Ellis Landing Beach

Point of Rocks
Landing Beach

Breakwater Beach

Saints Landing Beach

Robbins Hill Bch

Paine's Creek Beach

Crosby Ln.

Linnell

Ellis

Foster Rd.

Point of Rocks

Breakwater

Paine's
Creek

Lower Rd.

6A

Flax
Pond
Beach

Big
Cliff
Pond

Little
Cliff
Pond

Tubman
Rd.

124

Under-
pass Rd.

Millstone Rd.

NICKERSON
STATE
PARK

Stony Brook Rd

Run Hill Rd.

Great Fields Rd.

Long Pond Rd.

Freemans   Way

Setucket Rd.

W Gate Rd.

Upper Mill
Pond

Sheep
Pond

137

6

39

Slough
Pond Beach

Crowell Bog Rd.

Long Pond Beach

DENNIS

HARWICH

Big Cliff Pond

Flax Pond Road, Brewster • Nickerson State Park • 508.896.3491

     Parking fee is for all of Nickerson State Park. Boat rentals.
Note: This pond is sometimes closed due to algal blooms.

Breakwater Beach

Breakwater Road, Brewster • Cape Cod Bay • 508.896.4511

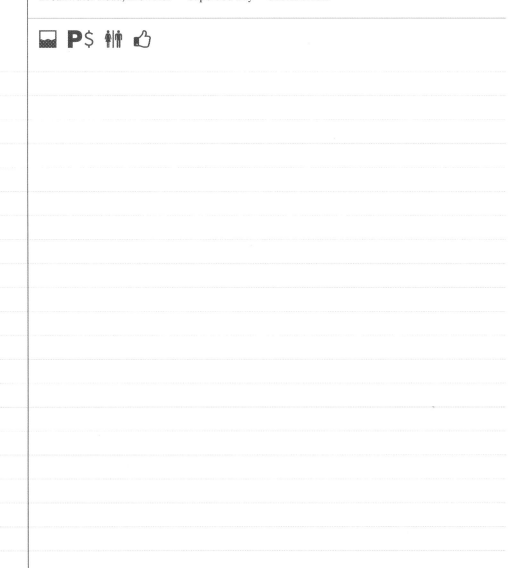

Crosby Landing Beach

Crosby Lane, Brewster • Cape Cod Bay • 508.896.4511

Ellis Landing Beach

Ellis Landing Road, Brewster • Cape Cod Bay • 508.896.4511

Flax Pond Beach

Flax Pond Road, Brewster • Nickerson State Park • 508.896.3491

 Parking fee is for all of Nickerson State Park. Boat rentals.

Linnell Landing Beach

Linnell Road, Brewster • Cape Cod Bay • 508.896.4511

Little Cliff Pond

Flax Pond Road, Brewster • Nickerson State Park • 508.896.3491

   Parking fee is for all of Nickerson State Park. Boat rentals.
Short walk through the woods to get there.

Long Pond Beach

Crowell's Bog Road, Brewster • 508.896.3491

Paine's Creek Beach

Paines Creek Road, Brewster • Cape Cod Bay • 508.896.4511

Point of Rocks Landing Beach

Point of Rocks Road, Brewster • Cape Cod Bay • 508.896.4511

Robbins Hill Beach (Mant's Landing)

Long Road, Brewster • Cape Cod Bay • 508.896.4511

Saints Landing Beach

Robbins Hill Road, Brewster • Cape Cod Bay • 508.896.4511

 P$

Sheep Pond

Fisherman's Landing Road, Brewster • 508.896.4511

Slough Pond Beach

Slough Road, Brewster • 508.896.4511

Upper Mill Pond

Old Run Hill Road, Brewster • 508.896.4511

   Tiny beach, mostly for boat launches.

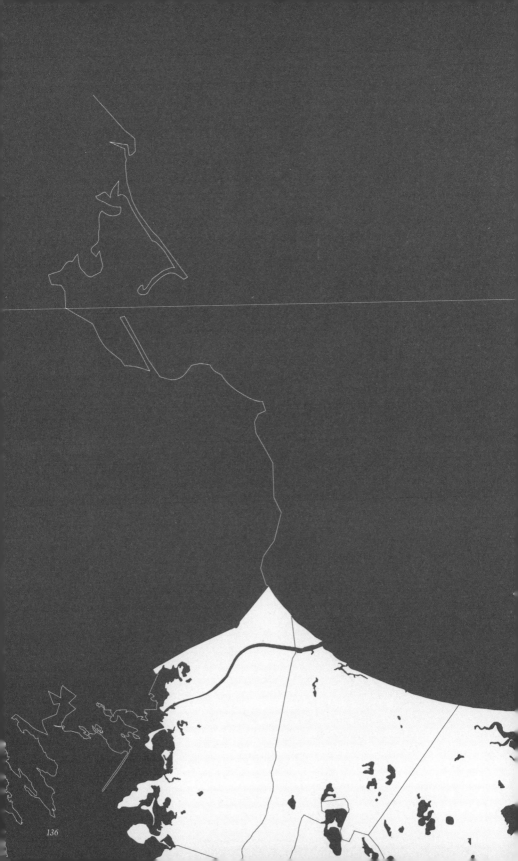

Outer Cape

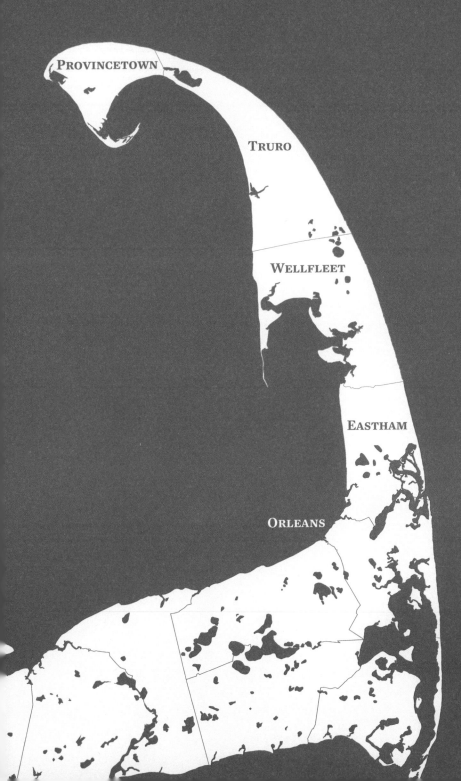

PROVINCETOWN

TRURO

WELLFLEET

EASTHAM

ORLEANS

Orleans

NOTES

Parking Fees — In effect from late May to late September.

Parking Stickers — Available to residents, renters, and visitors, sold on Nauset Beach.

Dogs — Not allowed on beaches April 1 through Labor Day.

MORE INFO + STICKERS
Parks & Beaches Department
139 Main Street
508.240.3775

STICKERS
Nauset Beach Admininistration
18 Bay Ridge Ln.
508.240.3780
Daily: 9AM–4PM

Cape Cod Bay

DENNIS

HARW

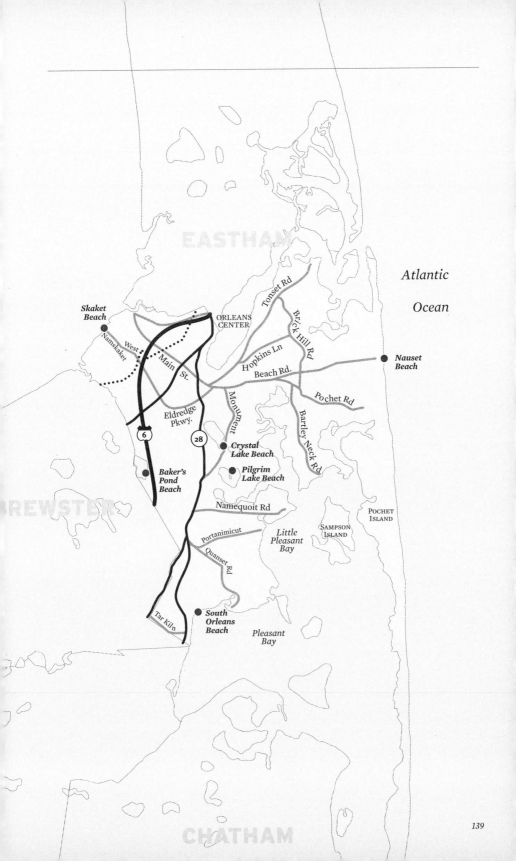

Atlantic

Ocean

Skaket
Beach

Namskaket

West

Main St.

ORLEANS
CENTER

Tonset Rd

Brick Hill Rd

Hopkins Ln

Beach Rd.

Nauset
Beach

Pochet Rd

Eldredge
Pkwy.

Monument

Barley Neck Rd

6

28

Crystal
Lake Beach

Baker's
Pond
Beach

Pilgrim
Lake Beach

Namequoit Rd

Portanimicut

Quanset Rd

Little
Pleasant
Bay

SAMPSON
ISLAND

POCHET
ISLAND

Tar Kiln

South
Orleans
Beach

Pleasant
Bay

EASTHAM

BREWSTER

CHATHAM

Baker's Pond Beach

Bakers Pond Road, off Rt. 6A, Orleans • 508.240.3775

State stocked pond for fishing. No combustion engines.

Crystal Lake Beach

Monument Road, Orleans • 508.240.3775

Handicapped ramp on the Route 28 side. State stocked pond for fishing. No combustion engines.

Nauset Beach

Beach Road, Orleans • Atlantic Ocean • 508.240.3775

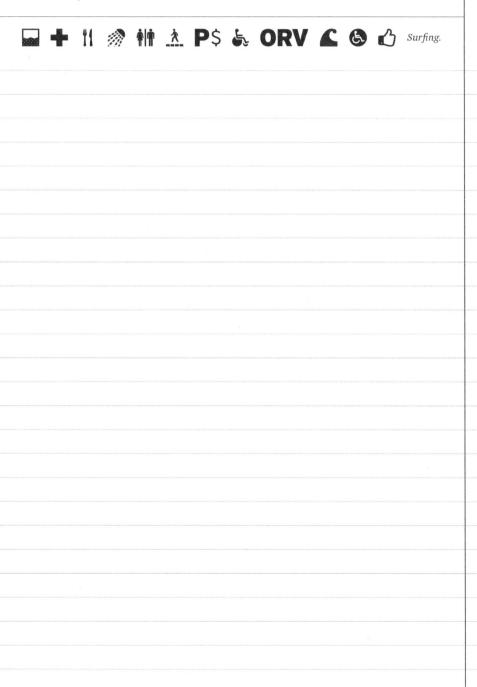 _Surfing._

Pilgrim Lake Beach

Herring Brook Road, Orleans • 508.240.3775

 *Fishing. Inflatables allowed. No combustion engines.*

Skaket Beach

West Road, Orleans • Cape Cod Bay • 508.240.3775

South Orleans Beach

Route 28, Orleans • Pleasant Bay, on Atlantic Ocean • 508.240.3775

 P

Eastham

NOTES

Eastham has both town-owned beaches and Cape Cod National Seashore beaches, which are operated by the federal government.

Parking Fees — In effect from late June through Labor Day, 9AM-4PM.

Parking Stickers — Open to residents and long-term renters.

Dogs — Not allowed on any of the town beaches at any time from June 15 through Labor Day.

MORE INFO
Recreation & Beaches
2500 State Highway
508.240.5974

**Cape Cod
National Seashore**
Parking: $20
Motorcycle parking: $10
Bike or foot access: $3
508.771.2144

STICKERS
**Natural Resources
Facility**
555 Old Orchard Rd.
508.240.5976
M–Sat: 9AM–4PM
Wed: 9AM–12PM

Wiley Park
Herring Brook Road
Sun: 9AM–4PM

Cape Cod Bay

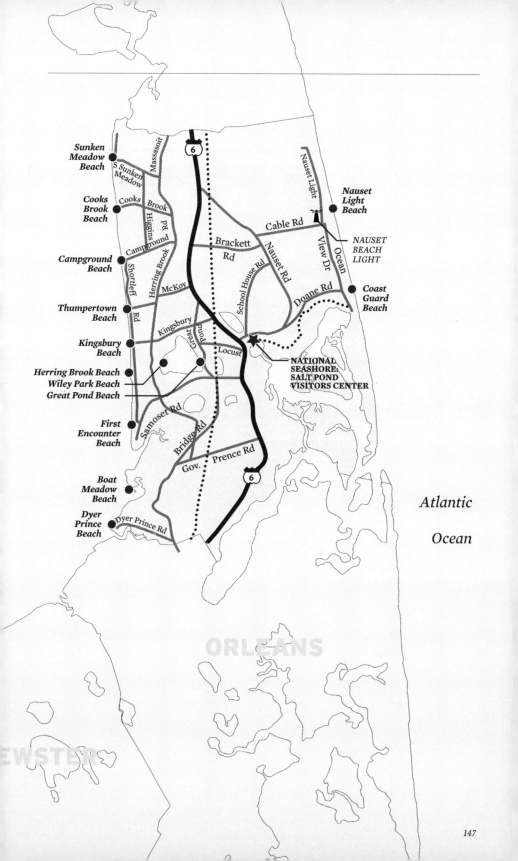

Sunken
Meadow
Beach

S Sunken
Meadow

Massasoit

Cooks
Brook
Beach

Cooks

Brook Rd

Higgins

Campground Beach

Campground

Shortleff Rd

Herring Brook

McKoy

Thumpertown
Beach

Kingsbury
Beach

Kingsbury

Great Pond

Locust

Herring Brook Beach
Wiley Park Beach
Great Pond Beach

Samoset Rd

First
Encounter
Beach

Bridge Rd

Boat
Meadow
Beach

Gov. Prence Rd

Dyer
Prince
Beach

Dyer Prince Rd

Brackett
Rd

School House Rd

Nauset Rd

Cable Rd

Nauset Light

View Dr

Ocean

Nauset
Light
Beach

NAUSET
BEACH
LIGHT

Doane Rd

Coast
Guard
Beach

★ NATIONAL
SEASHORE:
SALT POND
VISITORS CENTER

6

6

Atlantic

Ocean

ORLEANS

EWSTER

Boat Meadow Beach

Bayview Road, Eastham • Cape Cod Bay • 508.240.5976

   Not handicapped accessible.

Campground Beach

Campground Road, Eastham • Cape Cod Bay • 508.240.5976

Coast Guard Beach

Doane Road, Eastham • Cape Cod National Seashore • Atlantic Ocean • 508.487.6983

Fee for bicycles and pedestrians.
Long sloping ramp.

Cooks Brook Beach

Steele Road, Eastham • Cape Cod Bay • 508.240.5976

Dyer Prince Beach

Dyer Prince Road, Eastham • Cape Cod Bay • 508.240.5976

First Encounter Beach

Samoset Road, Eastham • Cape Cod Bay • 508.240.5976

 Call 508.240.5000 to reserve wheelchair.

Great Pond Beach

Great Pond Road, Eastham • 508.240.5976

Daily passes are valid, but must be purchased at one of the non-sticker beaches.

Herring Brook Beach

Cole Road, Eastham • Cape Cod Bay • 508.240.5976

Kingsbury Beach

Kingsbury Road, Eastham • Cape Cod Bay • 508.240.5976

Nauset Light Beach

Cable Road, Eastham • Cape Cod National Seashore • Atlantic Ocean • 508.487.6983

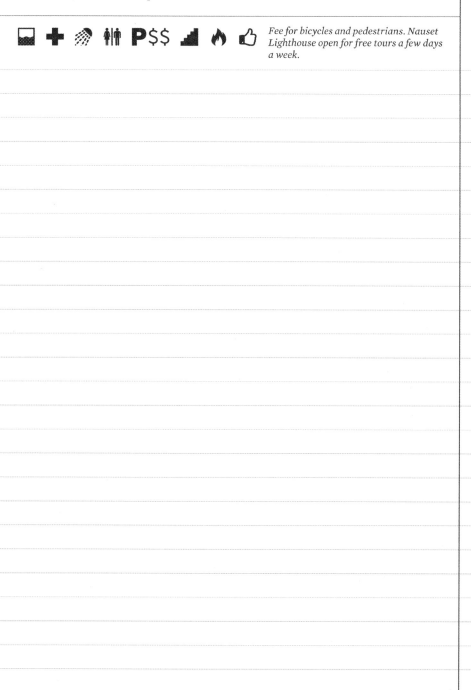

Fee for bicycles and pedestrians. Nauset Lighthouse open for free tours a few days a week.

Sunken Meadow Beach

South Sunken Meadow Road, Eastham • Cape Cod Bay • 508.240.5976

Thumpertown Beach

Thumpertown Road, Eastham • Cape Cod Bay • 508.240.5976

Wiley Park Beach

Herring Brook Road, Eastham • 508.240.5976

Wellfleet

Wellfleet has both town-owned beaches and beaches that are part of the Cape Cod National Seashore. Wellfleet is also one of the few towns that offers permits for beach campfires (after 6:30PM); call the Beach Sticker Office for more info.

Parking Stickers — Most of the Wellfleet beaches require a sticker for parking. Visitors can purchase temporary stickers, but will need to prove temporary residency in the town.

In effect from mid-June through Labor Day.

Dogs — From June 15 to Labor Day, dogs (leashed) are allowed in non-lifeguard areas on oceanside beaches only.

Camp Fires — Allowed on noted beaches with permit. Call Beach Sticker Office for more info.

MORE INFO
**Cape Cod
National Seashore**
Parking: $20
Motorcycle parking: $10
Bike or foot access: $3
508.771.2144

STICKERS
**Wellfleet Beach Sticker
Office**
508.349-9818
36 Shore Rd.
Route 6A
(Next to the North Truro Post Office)
Daily: 8:30AM–4:00PM

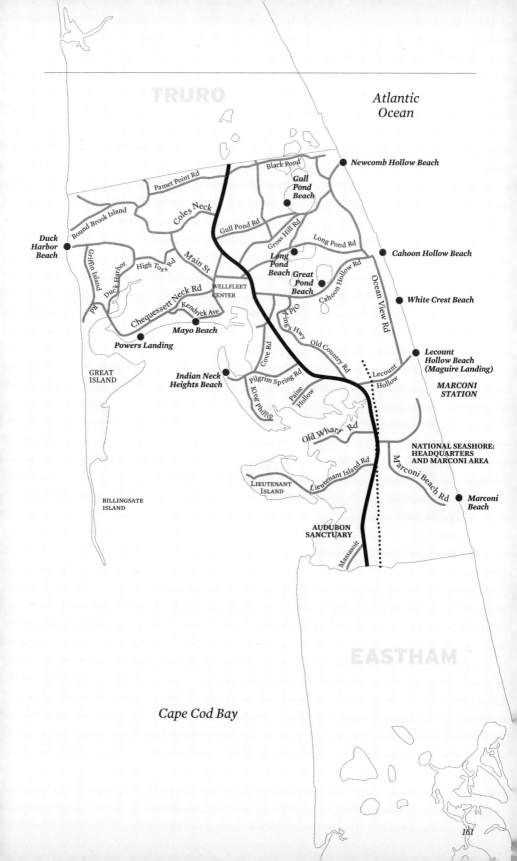

TRURO

Atlantic Ocean

Pamet Point Rd

Black Pond

● Newcomb Hollow Beach

Gull Pond Beach

Coles Neck

Gull Pond Rd

Gross Hill Rd

Bound Brook Island

Long Pond Rd

Duck Harbor Beach ●

Griffin Island

Duck Harbor

High Toss Rd

Main St

Long Pond Beach

● Cahoon Hollow Beach

Great Pond Beach

Cahoon Hollow Rd

● White Crest Beach

Chequessett Neck Rd

WELLFLEET CENTER

Ocean View Rd

Kendrick Ave

Old King's Hwy

Old Country Rd

● Mayo Beach

Cove Rd

Lecount Hollow Beach (Maguire Landing)

Powers Landing ●

Lecount Hollow

MARCONI STATION

GREAT ISLAND

Indian Neck Heights Beach ●

Pilgrim Spring Rd

Paine Hollow

King Phillip

Old Wharf Rd

NATIONAL SEASHORE: HEADQUARTERS AND MARCONI AREA

Marconi Beach Rd

BILLINGSATE ISLAND

LIEUTENANT ISLAND

Lieutenant Island Rd

● Marconi Beach

AUDUBON SANCTUARY

Massasoit

Cape Cod Bay

EASTHAM

Cahoon Hollow Beach

Cahoon Hollow Road, Wellfleet • Atlantic Ocean • 508.349.9818

Steep dune entrance. Can park at the Beachcomber for a fee and get a voucher to use in the restaurant.

Duck Harbor Beach

Duck Harbor Road, Wellfleet • Cape Cod Bay • 508.349.9818

Great Pond Beach

Cahoon Hollow Road, Wellfleet • 508.349.9818

    Shady. Very small.

Gull Pond Beach

Schoolhouse Road, Wellfleet • 508.349.9818

 *Very shady. Small.*

Indian Neck Heights Beach

Samoset Avenue, Wellfleet • Cape Cod Bay/Wellfleet Harbor • 508.349.9818

 *Windsurfing and sailboarding allowed.*

Lecount Hollow Beach (Maguire Landing)

Lecount Hollow Road, South Wellfleet • Atlantic Ocean • 508.349.9818

 *Steep dune entrance.*

Long Pond Beach

Long Pond Road, Wellfleet • 508.349.9818

    Shady.

Marconi Beach

Marconi Beach Road, South Wellfleet • Atlantic Ocean
Cape Cod National Seashore • 508.349.3785

 *Fee for bicycles and pedestrians.*

Mayo Beach

Kendrick Avenue, Wellfleet • Cape Cod Bay/Wellfleet Harbor • 508.349.9818

Playground and bathrooms across the street.
Call in advance to reserve beach wheelchair.

Newcomb Hollow Beach

Gross Hill Road, Wellfleet • Atlantic Ocean • 508.349.9818

Steep dune entrance. Very calm waves, compared to other Wellfleet ocean beaches.

Powers Landing

Off Chequessett Neck Road, Wellfleet • Cape Cod Bay/Wellfleet Harbor • 508.349.9818

White Crest Beach

Ocean View Drive, Wellfleet • Atlantic Ocean • 508.349.9818

Truro

PROVINCETOW

NOTES

Truro has both town-owned beaches and beaches that are part of the Cape Cod National Seashore.

Parking Stickers — All but two of the Truro beaches require a sticker for parking from mid-June through Labor Day. Visitors can purchase temporary stickers, but will need to prove temporary residency in the town.

Lifeguards — None of the bay beaches offer lifeguards.

Fire Permits and Off Road Vehicle Permits — Several beaches offer beach fire permits and off road vehicle permits. More information available through the Beach Office or the relevant agencies on the right.

Dogs — Allowed on beaches before 9AM and after 6PM.

STICKERS + MORE INFO
**Cape Cod
National Seashore**
Parking: $20
Motorcycle parking: $10
Bike or foot access: $3
508.771.2144

Truro Beach Office
36 Shore Rd.
North Truro (Rt 6A)
508.487.6983

FIRE PERMITS
Truro Fire Department
508.487.7548

ORV LICENSING DESK
Truro Town Hall
24 Town Hall Rd.
M–F: 8:00AM–4:00PM

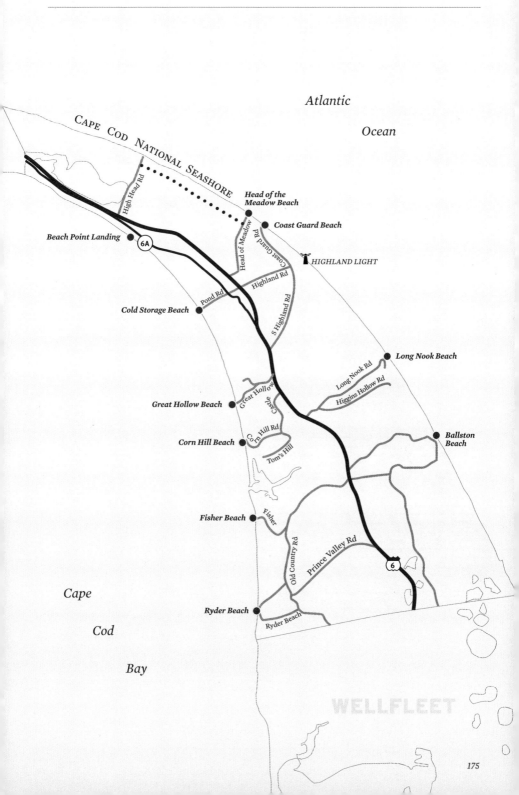

Atlantic

Ocean

CAPE COD NATIONAL SEASHORE

High Head Rd

Head of the
Meadow Beach

Beach Point Landing

Coast Guard Beach

6A

HIGHLAND LIGHT

Head of Meadow Rd

Coast Guard Rd

Highland Rd

Pond Rd

Cold Storage Beach

S Highland Rd

Long Nook Beach

Long Nook Rd

Great Hollow

Higgins Hollow Rd

Great Hollow Beach

Castle

Corn Hill Rd

Ballston
Beach

Corn Hill Beach

Tom's Hill

Fisher Beach

Fisher

Old Country Rd

Prince Valley Rd

6

Cape

Cod

Ryder Beach

Ryder Beach

Bay

WELLFLEET

Ballston Beach

North Pamet Road, Truro • Atlantic Ocean • 508.487.6983

    Not very handicap accessible.

Beach Point Landing

Shore Road, Route 6A, Truro • Cape Cod Bay • 508.487.6983

Coast Guard Beach

Coast Guard Road, Truro • Atlantic Ocean • 508.487.6983

    Not very handicap accessible. Note that there is another Coast Guard Beach in Eastham.

Cold Storage Beach (Pond Village Beach)

Pond Road, North Truro • Cape Cod Bay • 508.487.6983

🛏 🕴 Ⓢ *Not handicap accessible.*

Corn Hill Beach

Corn Hill Road, Truro • Cape Cod Bay • 508.487.6983

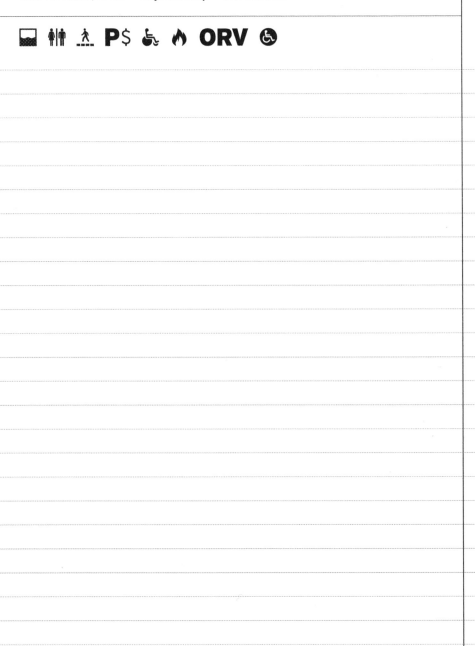

Fisher Beach

Fisher Road, Truro • Cape Cod Bay • 508.487.6983

 *Not very accessible.*

Great Hollow Beach

Great Hollow Road, Truro • Cape Cod Bay • 508.487.6983

     Popular for kayaking.

Head of the Meadow Beach

Head of the Meadow Road, Truro • Atlantic Ocean • 508.487.6983
(There are two separate beaches with separate lots and amenities.)

CCNS beach: 🏖 ➕ 🚿 🚻 **P$$** 🔥   *Fee for bicycles and pedestrians.*

Town beach: 🏖 ➕ 🔥 **P$** ♿ ♿

Long Nook Beach

Long Nook Road, Truro • Atlantic Ocean • 508.487.6983

    Nude sunbathing at the edges.

Ryder Beach

Ryder Beach Road, Truro • Cape Cod Bay • 508.487.6983

Provincetown

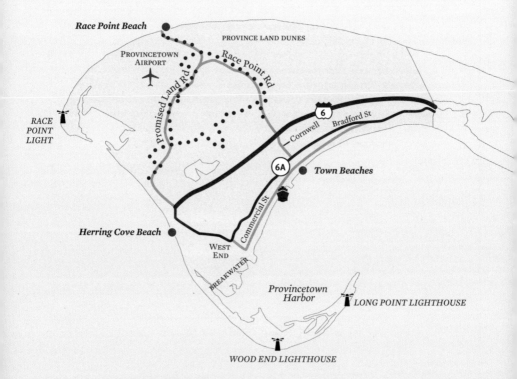

Atlantic Ocean

Race Point Beach

PROVINCE LAND DUNES

PROVINCETOWN AIRPORT

Race Point Rd

Promised Land Rd

RACE POINT LIGHT

6

Cornwell

Bradford St

6A

Town Beaches

Commercial St

Herring Cove Beach

WEST END

BREAKWATER

Provincetown Harbor

LONG POINT LIGHTHOUSE

WOOD END LIGHTHOUSE

Cape Cod Bay

Provincetown's main beaches are part of the Cape Cod National Seashore. A number of small town beaches run parallel to Commercial St. These are not great swimming beaches, but pleasant to walk along. Amenities such as bathrooms and food are available along Commercial St.

The Provincetown Shuttle offers access to both Race Point and Herring Cove Beaches.

Dogs — Dogs are allowed on beaches outside of lifeguard-protected areas and bird-nesting zones. They are also allowed on seashore fire roads, the Head of the Meadow Bicycle Trail (year-round), Province Lands Bicycle Trail (from Nov. 1–April 30), and seashore freshwater ponds (Oct. 16–May 14).

STICKERS + MORE INFO
**Cape Cod
National Seashore**
Parking: $20
Motorcycle parking: $10
Bike or foot access: $3
508.771.2144

TRURO

Herring Cove Beach

Race Point Road, Provincetown • Cape Cod National Seashore • Cape Cod Bay
866.355.3266

 *Fee for bicycles and pedestrians. Provincetown shuttle access.*

Race Point Beach

Race Point Road, Provincetown • Cape Cod National Seashore
Cape Cod Bay/Atlantic Ocean • 508.349.3785

Fee for bicycles and pedestrians.
Provincetown shuttle access.

Town Beaches

Along Commercial Street, the length of the village.
Look for alleys leading to the beaches • Provincetown Harbor

*The closest amenities are nearby on Commerical St. Not great swimming beaches.
The best one for swimming is the West End Beach, towards the breakwater.*

Index